The Work of the Clerk

New Edition

1-23/06

Hi Babe,

This is The guide
line that I have
been following.
This was given to me
by The first Pastor That
I serbed under.
I am now on
Pastor #3 with
the Same guide.

Edit

The Work of the Clerk
New Edition

M. Ingrid Dvirnak

Judson Press ® Valley Forge

The Work of the Clerk, New Edition
© 1996 Judson Press, Valley Forge, PA 19482-0851

Library of Congress Cataloging-in-Publication Data
Dvirnak, M. Ingrid
   The work of the clerk / M. Ingrid Dvirnak. -- New ed.
p.   cm.
   Rev. ed. of: The work of the clerk / Zelotes Grenell and Agnes Grenell Goss. 1967.
    ISBN 0-8170-1253-2 (pbk.)
    1. Church officers. I. Grenell, Zelotes, 1841-1918. The work of the clerk. II. Title.
BV705.D85 1996
254--dc20   96-11400

Printed in the U.S.A.
05
10 9 8 7 6 5 4 3

Contents

Preface vii

Acknowledgments ix

Chapter 1
Profile of an Effective Clerk 1

Chapter 2
The Clerk as Recorder 7

Chapter 3
The Clerk as Historian 25

Chapter 4
The Clerk as Correspondent 31

Chapter 5
The Clerk as Publicist 35

Conclusion 39

Related Resources 41

Additional Church Record Resources. . . . 49

Preface

For almost ninety years, church clerks have been using this handbook to help them do their work. First printed in 1909, *The Work of the Clerk* has served as a valuable resource to church clerks in many denominations. Zelotes Grenell, the original author, and Agnes Grenell Goss, who revised her father's manuscript in 1967, have made significant contributions to local church ministry. Through their writing, they, in turn, have enabled and inspired church clerks to make lasting contributions.

The current revision brings *The Work of the Clerk* into the computer age. Along with helpful suggestions for the use of word processors and databases, this book incorporates advice from people serving as clerks in local churches. Their insights are valuable because they go beyond theory to what really works.

As a clergy spouse, I appreciate the conscientious work of church clerks. Accurate records are important. Just ask anyone whose receipt of Social Security depends on a church clerk's verification of a baptismal date. Or the person who wants to know more about family history. Or the church member who seeks information about a significant decision in the life of the church. As the church clerk, you are the person to whom they will come. It is for you that this book is written.

—*M. Ingrid Dvirnak*
October 1995

Acknowledgments

I am grateful to Ronald Cowles, executive minister of the American Baptist Churches of the Dakotas, for supplying the names of currently active church clerks for me to interview. Their candid responses to my questions have been valuable.

Some of the clerks I interviewed had stories to tell. I have incorporated several into the manuscript. Where feasible, their actual names have been used to identify them.

Special thanks to Doris Rongley, who has had many years of experience doing the work of the clerk, and to Deb Greenup, a newly elected church clerk, for reading the manuscript and providing practical insights. Betty Layton, archivist at the American Baptist Historical Society, provided assistance with the content of the chapter entitled "The Clerk as Historian."

As has been true with all my writing projects, my husband, Wayne, is my principal encourager and critic. I place great value on his contributions, not the least of which is a creative climate in which to work.

Chapter 1

Profile of an Effective Clerk

If you are reading this book, you probably already have been elected to the position of church clerk. Perhaps the nominating committee looked at the clerk's job description and drew up a list of preferred characteristics. Their list led them to you. You were interested in a new challenge. You agreed to place your name in nomination, so congratulations are now in order.

Or perhaps you found yourself in a different scenario. Maybe you were asked to serve because "there isn't much to the job" or "we can't seem to find anyone else who wants to do it." Or even worse, you were a warm body occupying space at the recent business session. On the slate of officers to be elected, the slot marked "church clerk" was still open. You were nominated from the floor of the business session and didn't have a clue about all the job entailed. Thinking that further deliberation might appear discourteous, your friend made the motion to close nominations, so you were elected by a unanimous vote. Clerks come to the position in a variety of ways. Let's look at a desirable process model.

The Nominating Committee's Preview

When the nominating committee meets to find nominees for the year ahead or to fill vacancies that occur between annual meetings, they have an important job to do. They must match the needs of the organization to the gifts of its members and then secure willing nominees to present to the body for election.

As the committee begins to consider possible nominees for the church clerk, they determine that they are looking for a member who is:

- in regular attendance at church functions;
- interested in the work of the church and denomination;
- able to work well with others;
- organized;
- a clear communicator who possesses skills in both written and oral media;
- detail oriented;
- prompt; and
- willing to give time to the assigned tasks.

After the committee looks over the list of members (which has been provided for their use by the current clerk) and looks for complementary information in the church's skills/gifts/talents bank (where available), they find names of several prospective nominees. Committee members then prioritize their list of names. Someone agrees to visit with the first person on the list. During this personal visit, the nominating committee member explains the work of the clerk by sharing information found in the clerk's job description and references to the clerk in the church's constitution or bylaws.

Maybe it happened this way for you. Maybe it didn't. Regardless, you have consented to serve a term as the clerk in your church, and you want to do a good job. You are looking forward to your task with eagerness. A closer examination of the job qualifications will give you a glimpse at the work ahead of you.

Attends Church Regularly

The clerk should be someone who attends church regularly. The clerk records events that take place in the life of the church. These events include not only business sessions but also events of a historical nature. In some cases, the clerk is also the congregation's publicity agent. It is important that the clerk be an active member of the church family.

Exhibits an Interest in the Church and Denomination

The congregation's record keeper, the clerk, is vested with the responsibility of filling out annual denominational reports. Up-to-date church records make the filling out of year-end reports a rewarding experience. Just as the church depends on the clerk to keep accurate records of the year's events, so regional and national denominational offices depend on local churches to supply accurate reports of their progress during the year. The key person in this process is the clerk.

Works Well with Others

The clerk is a team player. Working closely with the pastor, the moderator, and other church officers, the clerk experiences the exhilaration of contributing to a common cause—God's kingdom work being accomplished through the local church and its extended family. The clerk is dependent on others while being keenly aware of others' mutual dependency. While the clerk's role is individual and unique, interaction is essential to getting the job done.

Possesses Organizational Skills

The very nature of record keeping calls for organization. Minutes must be concise; membership rolls must be accurate. Publicity must answer the "who," "what," "where," "when," "why," and "how" questions. Likewise, letters written on behalf of the congregation must be clear.

Is a Skilled Communicator

Much of the clerk's work is written communication. It takes the form of correspondence, minutes, reports, historical notations, and press releases. While the bulk of the clerk's work is done on paper, it is not limited to written words. An oral reading of the minutes is often requested by the moderator.

Appreciates the Significance of Details

When baby Elise is born to someone involved in the life of the congregation, the clerk records the date of birth in the church records. When she is baptized, the event is recorded. The day she becomes a member of the church as well as the day she joins her life with another in marriage are written down. Should she decide to move her membership to another church, that transfer is duly recorded. At the end of her life, the date of her death is entered into her congregation's register. Exact dates are vital to these individual minibiographies.

In the same way, motions are critical elements in the minutes of business meetings, and facts are integral to historical journals. For the clerk, and for the persons who depend on the work of the clerk, details are important.

Performs Tasks Promptly

Following closely on the heels of the importance of details is the need for promptness. The person who serves as the clerk should be a person who is accustomed to doing things right and on time. Many clerks who were interviewed in preparation for the writing of this revised edition gave this advice: "Keep your books up to date."

Commits Quality Time to the Task

Joe, a clerk in a small church in the Midwest, suggests that it's easiest to sit down on Sunday afternoon or evening and write down all that happened on that day and during the previous week. Whether Sunday is "the" day or not is immaterial. What *is* important is that the clerk schedules time on a regular basis to do the required work.

Now, as you interact with the following pages that describe your work in detail, think about the qualities described in this chapter. Some of these qualities you already possess; others you know you need to cultivate. Focus on your good points. Work to improve your weaker points. In doing so, you will be an effective clerk.

Chapter 2

The Clerk as Recorder

Church clerks write the church's biography. Much more than minutes of meetings and collections of names and dates, the clerk's records become an interesting story. They display benchmarks, in convenient reference form, against which the growth and development of a church may be measured.

These are the records many pastors use upon arrival at a church in order to get a feel for their new ministry setting. The clerk's records provide essential information upon which future generations will look in joyous celebration.

If a church is incorporated, the law considers the clerk to be the corporation's secretary. Minutes are the official and legal record of an organization. The courts may rely on the clerk's records to determine the truth in specific situations. In all of these cases, accuracy is of primary importance. The clerk's records must tell the truth in an understandable fashion.

Recording the Minutes

Every regular and special meeting of the church generates a set of minutes. During the meeting, the clerk makes notes of what happens. As soon as is possible after the meeting, these notes should be transcribed. Copies should be distributed at least to the pastor and moderator for their use in preparing for the next meeting where the minutes will be presented for approval. Upon approval, the minutes are then entered into the permanent record. Exactly how this happens is up to you and the structures and traditions of your church.

During business sessions, sit where you can see and hear everything. You may want to be seated at a small table near the moderator. In this position, you are easily seen and heard when called upon to read, and you can conveniently confer with the moderator as needed.

Your equipment at the meeting should suit your personal style. Paper and pen or pencil are requisites. The constitution and bylaws, a church directory, and a list of officers and board/committee members are useful reference items. Keep a copy of each one handy during meetings.

Some people have acquired the skill of recording their business meeting notes on a laptop computer. Of course, your laptop should be equipped with the word processing program you know best. If you use a laptop, make provision for the possibility of technical difficulties. Carry the old standby supplies "just in case."

Using a laptop computer during the business session makes transcription easy. After the meeting, you need only expand your abbreviations, check your spelling, insert the appropriate headings, and print a copy to proofread. Otherwise, type or prepare a handwritten copy of the minutes. If you prepare the minutes on a desktop computer, save a copy of your file on a disk and note its location so you can easily return to it and make the necessary corrections.

In some churches where a secretary is employed, it is the secretary's job to prepare the final copy of the minutes, especially if the clerk does not have access to a typewriter or computer. However, as a courtesy to the secretary, prepare a complete draft of the minutes. Don't expect the secretary to decipher your abbreviated notes. As clerk, you are responsible for the accurate written record of the church's business.

If a friend or family member is willing to proofread your minutes, take advantage of their gift to you. Any errors they find or clarifying questions they ask will reduce the number of corrections made during the business session where you will present the minutes for approval.

For computer users, correcting errors is easy. Simply go back through the file, make the corrections, and print out a new hard copy. At this point, remember to save the corrected file to a disk. Make a note of the file name and its directory so you can easily access it again.

If you are writing or typing, clean copies should be the norm. Minimal corrections may be made with opaque correction fluid or correction tape. Crossed-out letters, words, or sentences are unacceptable.

After the minutes have been proofread and corrected, make copies and distribute them. It has already been mentioned that the moderator and pastor should receive a copy soon after the meeting. There may be other people who should receive copies; confer with the moderator and pastor to determine who they are. In some churches, minutes are also displayed on the bulletin board.

The moderator may ask you to prepare a list of unfinished items of business to be included on the next meeting's agenda. Your clear record keeping will make this task uncomplicated.

One of the first items of business at the next meeting will be the approval of your minutes. Be prepared to read your minutes aloud or to distribute copies at the beginning of the session. If you are unsure which method will be used, ask the moderator or pastor. After the minutes are approved as read or as corrected, they are ready to be added to the permanent record. You should have received this book from your predecessor. If you did not, ask the moderator or pastor where the book is kept.

The Contents of the Minutes

Do

Begin with the time, date, type of meeting (regular, special, annual), call to order, and the name of the presiding officer.

Record a quorum count.

Include the exact wording of a proposed motion. If you are unsure, ask for a written copy or ask to have it repeated while you write it down word for word. Edit only superficial errors such as grammar or spelling. Record the name of the person making a motion and whether the motion was adopted or rejected. If the vote is by ballot, enter the number of votes on each side.

Don't

Record the place of the meeting when the place is always the same, for example, the church fellowship hall.

Include names of everyone present.

Enter the name of the person who seconds a motion.

Do

Be brief. Be specific. Be accurate. Simply record the proceedings of the meeting.

File committee reports with the minutes. If reports contain recommendations on which the body takes action, record the action taken.

Allot one paragraph for each item of business. Leave a wide left margin for notes to identify the items. People who use the minutes for reference will appreciate clear identification of each issue dealt with during the meeting.

Don't

Describe your personal interpretations of the business proceedings. Words that mirror your own mood or opinion are inappropriate.

Include the full contents of reports in the minutes. In some cases, a report may be considered to be unusually important, and the body orders the report to be entered into the minutes. In that instance, you would be required to copy the entire report into your minutes.

Record all new business or all old business in one paragraph. People who refer to minutes in the future will find it difficult to locate specific issues and decisions.

Sample Minutes

Call to Order	The quarterly business meeting was called to order by Dean Sanders, moderator, on Wednesday evening, January 10, 1996. Rev. Janis Swift led in prayer.
Quorum Count	It was determined that a quorum was present.
Secretary's Minutes	The minutes of the previous meeting were read and approved.
Treasurer's Report	A treasurer's report was distributed and filed with the minutes.
New Members Received	Upon recommendation of the Diaconate, Phil Cameron moved that the following people be received as members pending the receipt of their letters of transfer: Leigh Evans, Frank Griffin, John Larson, and Sue Paine. Motion carried.
New Pew Bibles	Upon recommendation of the Board of Christian Education, Marcia Finley moved that $575

be approved for the purchase of New Revised Standard Version Bibles for the pews. Motion carried.

Trustees Report

Cal Sorenson reported on the progress being made toward the purchase of a new van. No action was required. The report was received; a copy is filed with the minutes.

Clergy Sabbatical

Upon recommendation of the Pastoral Relations Committee, Sylvia Connors moved that Rev. Swift be given a three-month sabbatical in appreciation for six years of ministry with our congregation. The sabbatical will begin June 1, 1996, and continue through August 31, 1996. Motion carried.

Adjournment

The meeting was adjourned with several members offering prayers of thanks for Rev. Swift's ministry among us.

Respectfully submitted,
Jim Wilkinson, Clerk

Recording Amendments to the Constitution, Bylaws, or Standing Rules

An amendment to the church constitution, bylaws, or standing rules should be immediately entered into the document of which it is a part. If these documents are on a computer, the changes are easily and quickly made. Before saving the changes on the computer, be sure to print out a hard copy of the document as it appeared before the amendment was made. Or show the changes in the document by indicating new text in **bold** print and deleted text in ~~strike-through~~ print. Create a parenthetical or marginal note indicating the date and page of the minutes where the action to amend is recorded. At a later date, when a revised copy of the document is distributed to the membership, clean up the text, printing only the text as amended.

If the documents are typewritten or handwritten, every other page should remain blank. The amendments, along with a reference to the date and page of the minutes where the decision is recorded, should be written opposite the article amended.

Recording Membership Statistics

From the day your church was organized, it is likely that someone in the congregation has maintained membership rolls. The people whose names appear on those rolls *are* the church! The membership list forms the database for church mailings, stewardship campaigns, congregational profiles, denominational reports, and strategic mapping. An accurate, current membership list is necessary in order for the church to function efficiently and effectively.

For ease of reference, two types of lists are suggested: chronological and alphabetical. The chronological list is usually considered to be the *official* roll of the church. This list, often kept in a bound volume, should have been given to you when you began serving as the clerk. If not, it may be kept at the church. Ask to see it.

Both chronological and alphabetical lists are easily generated by using computer software specifically designed to manage church records. Most church management computer systems allow you to organize a membership database according to your local church's needs. They enable you to prepare customized reports and lists that contain the information and page formats that work best for you.

In addition to creating your reports and keeping your records organized, church management software packages also make other record-keeping tasks easier. Church management systems will:

- generate mailing labels for general and targeted mailings as needed by the church

office, officers, teachers, small group
leaders, and so on;

- compile complete congregational statistics
  quickly;
- provide the pastor and diaconate with
  names and addresses for visitation;
- assist in special outreach efforts by
  pinpointing ministry groups;
- format age and gender-grouping lists for
  the Christian education department and
  auxiliary organizations;
- track attendance, pledges, and financial
  contributions;
- maintain a skills and activities bank to
  facilitate effective use of gifts and abilities;
- reduce time spent in personalizing church
  correspondence;
- inventory equipment;
- store titles of music and books in the
  respective libraries; and
- build a library of past sermon titles and
  related subject and text information.

Record-keeping software is a good investment
that will enhance the work of the entire church.
The keys to its success, of course, are the trained
persons who use it. Contact your local software
supplier for details, demonstrations, trial systems,

and on-site training. Most systems sell for less than five hundred dollars.

The Makings of a Membership List

Both chronological and alphabetical membership lists should be tabular in format. Include the name of each member along with the date and manner of admission to the church. Where applicable, show the date and manner of dismission.

Begin each entry with the person's last name, followed by the full given name. Nicknames are not appropriate.

When a single woman marries, add her married name to the original entry. In the case of a married woman, use her own first name. Her husband's name or initials may be entered in parentheses following hers, if preferred. If you include titles, use the guidelines commonly accepted in your community.

Each entry should be complete in itself. Where several family members are entered consecutively, do not use ditto marks. Write each person's name in full.

Names of people who no longer belong to the church should not be removed. Instead, indicate the date and manner of dismission.

Guidelines for alphabetical membership lists are similar to those suggested for chronological lists. However, when a single woman marries, her new name should be placed in its proper alphabetical order. Since there are many ways alphabetical lists are used in church administration, include members' complete addresses and telephone numbers.

The alphabetical list needs to be rewritten or revised annually to keep it accurate. Many churches print and distribute an expanded alphabetical list to members and friends. In this form, the list usually includes nonmembers who call the church their home but who have not joined the family. It becomes a valuable source of information to all who have access to it.

In many instances, the office secretary prepares this resource for distribution. Of necessity, it must be done in consultation with the clerk. A convenient format for this alphabetical list in the church office is the rotary card file. Sometimes these cards also include space for church activity information, interests, skills, elected positions, and other responsibilities. With these additions, the alphabetical membership card file becomes a useful resource for the pastor and other church leaders.

Following are samples showing a membership card for an alphabetical file, a chronological membership list, and an alphabetical membership list.

Sample Membership Card for Alphabetical File
Church Membership Card

Name _____

Telephone Number _____

Address _____

City _____ State _____ Zip _____

Received   Date _____

By ____ Baptism

____ Experience

____ Letter from (church, city, and state)

____ Reinstatment/Restoration

Dismissed   Date _____

By ____ Letter to (church, city, and state)

____ Member's Own Request

____ Exclusion (Disciplinary Action by the
Congregation)

____ Death*

* For a fuller discussion of these terms, see Norman H.
Maring, *A Baptist Manual of Polity and Practice, Rev. Ed.*
(Valley Forge, Pa.: Judson Press, 1991), 72.

Sample Segment of a Chronological Membership List

Name	When/How Received	When/How Dismissed
Anderson, Ellie		
Babcock, James		
Babcock, Sarah		
Dodge, Maxwell		6/17/73 Letter
Fischer, Raymond		
Horton, Mary		11/29/80 Death
Jackson, George	6/15/69	
Mansfield, Diane	Charter Member	
Mansfield, Herb		
Mansfield, Kali		
Mansfield, Kent		
Patterson, Frank		
Patterson, Judy		
Steiner, Marshall		3/6/94 Request
McArthur, Paul	5/24/70 Baptism	
Norris, Brenda	5/24/70 Baptism	
Prentice, Angela	5/24/70 Baptism	
Benton, Doyle	8/16/70 Experience	
Kaufman, Harry	8/16/70 Letter	
Kaufman, Marilyn	8/16/70 Letter	
Kaufman, Tom	8/16/70 Letter	1/4/75 Letter
Kaufman, Wanda	8/16/70 Letter	6/5/73 Letter
Holte, Danielle	8/16/70 Letter	9/7/94 Request
Stevenson, Ellen	4/18/71 Experience	
Lohman, Bill	4/18/71 Baptism	
Lohman, Fern	4/18/71 Baptism	
Cleveland, Myrna	6/25/72 Baptism	2/8/75 Death

Sample Segment of an Alphabetical Membership List

Name	Born	Married	When/How Received	When/How Dismissed
Alton, Bruce			7/16/89 Letter	
Bishop, Chester			2/8/76 Baptism	
Cross, Jan			8/17/80 Letter	7/6/94 Request
Devane, Cathy			6/8/75 Letter	
Devane, Julie	3/29/77		7/12/91 Baptism	
Devane, Martin			6/8/75 Letter	
Evans, Lawrence		6/20/80	4/14/74 Baptism	
Evans, Lois		6/20/80	9/21/80 Letter	
Faulkner, Benita			1/12/75 Experience	
Johnson, Greta			6/28/81 Letter	
Johnson, Jim			6/28/81 Letter	
Johnson, Marci	8/1/83		7/16/95 Baptism	
Johnson, Vicki	6/29/81		12/4/94 Baptism	
Kenzler, Dolores			10/8/95 Experience	
Kenzler, Fred			10/8/95 Experience	
Maroni, Chet			5/16/71 Letter	11/13/82 Death

Preparing the Annual Report

An effective way to present a picture of the past year in the life of the congregation is to prepare a compilation of reports from each board or committee. The clerk's annual report includes a summary of the changes in membership: new members and the categories by which they were received, dismissed members and categories by which the membership decreased (such as transfers and deaths), the net increase/decrease, and a current total.

Unless a separate committee has been appointed, the clerk may also be responsible to collect report data from other officers and committee or board chairpersons. In other churches, the office secretary compiles, reproduces, and distributes the report.

Consider adding this special touch to your church's annual report book. Dedicate each year's edition to those members who have died during the previous twelve months. Marilyn's church does this, and it's her job as clerk to write a short sketch about each person. She includes the date the deceased joined the church, the offices the person held, and a few personal words of tribute. She recommends it as a special way of honoring and remembering loved ones.

Preparing Denominational Reports

The clerk assists in preparing denominational reports. These are usually requested annually and consist primarily of statistical information and officers' names and addresses for regional directory updates. The prompt gathering of accurate information is critical.

You will be able to obtain some of the statistics from the membership records and official minutes you have prepared during the past year. For example, you have easy access to the total number of current members. However, if you are asked to give a breakdown of the members according to age, for example, you may have to get those numbers from the Sunday church school secretary. So the annual report to the denomination becomes a team effort. Consult with other leaders:

- the treasurer or trustees for budgetary facts;
- women's and men's ministries presidents for gender-group information;
- youth advisors and children's workers for data that is age specific; and
- the pastor for answers to questions about the overall ministry and outreach of the church.

Regional and national leaders use the statistics from these reports in many ways. Facts and figures you submit become part of your church's permanent file. They are often examined closely by persons seeking pastoral placement. Goals are set, projections are created, trends are studied, decisions are made, and, yes, history is written on the basis of your accurate and prompt reporting.

Chapter 3

The Clerk as Historian

Church life is more than recorded facts and statistics. It is a collection of family events: sometimes celebrative, sometimes sobering—always historical. Unless someone else is specifically designated as the church historian, the recording of historical data falls among the duties of the clerk. In this role, the clerk not only records the business of the church but also tells the continuing story of the church family.

If this part of the job just doesn't seem to "fit" you, talk to the pastor and moderator about the possibility of delegating this task. Oftentimes, a longtime member would be honored to serve as the historian.

Church history commonly combines four forms of media: visual, written, and oral records, and material artifacts. However, for our purposes in this manual, we will take a look at the two forms most often undertaken by the church clerk: visual (church albums) and written (journal entries) record keeping.

The Church Album

A well-kept album is a treasure. A combination of visual and written records, it becomes an effective teaching tool to use with new members of all ages. It is also a valuable resource to which many will refer when they compile church anniversary booklets and historical pieces for the church newsletter. Look at the album as a supplement to the official records of the church.

Archivists discourage the use of a traditional "scrapbook" format for two reasons. Generally, scrapbooks are composed of poor quality, highly acidic paper. In addition, items in the book are secured with glue, paste, or tape, none of which are recommended by preservationists. If your church has kept scrapbooks in the past, consider changing to an album format.

Purchase an album with archivally safe, acid-free sleeves. Insert items in the sleeves for temporary display. Remove the items later and preserve them in the church's historical files.

Keep your church's history alive. Save the following items for your church's album:

- photographs, dated and clearly identified, of changes in the church building, of the minister(s) and other staff persons, of people and groups;
- award certificates received by the congregation;
- noteworthy correspondence related to special occasions;
- bulletins revealing significant change in the style of worship;
- samples of church publications, especially those that exhibit varying formats and philosophies;
- printed programs from special events;
- newspaper articles about church activities, as well as news items referring to members of the congregation. Since newsprint is not durable, photocopies of newspaper articles are better than the originals. This is true for any item printed on acidic paper, which yellows, becomes brittle, and eventually deteriorates.

Journal Entries

Writing history can be rewarding work. This was Violet's assessment as she helped her church prepare to celebrate its one hundredth anniversary. She began by reading the records kept by previous clerks, and then helped write the anniversary

booklet commissioned by the committee in charge
of the celebration. "It was rewarding to me," she
said. "Both present and past members enjoyed
having personal copies of the written history of
their home church."

The records she used to compile the booklet
may have been similar to these:

- May 22, 1994: Our pastor, Jim Ellison,
  received his license to preach the gospel of
  Jesus Christ. Following Pastor Jim's
  Pentecost sermon on the power of the Holy
  Spirit, the associate executive minister,
  Rose Becklin, addressed both the
  congregation and the pastor. Then she
  presented Pastor Jim with a certificate of
  license. A special coffee hour in honor of the
  Ellisons was hosted by the deacons
  following the morning service.
- September 25, 1994: Moderator Phyllis
  Bliss announced that Pastor Jim has met
  with the Ministerial Leadership
  Commission of our Region to begin the
  process of ordination. Pastor Jim plans to
  complete his biblical studies program at
  the end of this calendar year. After he
  prepares his doctrinal statement and
  presents it to the Commission for approval,
  we will host the meeting of the ordination
  council. The target date is summer 1995.

> Members of the congregation offered prayers of thanksgiving and support for Pastor Jim and his family as he pursues ordination.
>
> - July 7, 1995: The regional ordination council met and recommended our pastor, Jim Ellison, for ordination.
> - July 9, 1995: Jim Ellison was ordained. Special guests included many out-of-state relatives of the Ellisons and friends from eight sister churches. The ordination sermon was delivered by Dr. Allen Bidwell, our executive minister. The ceremony of ordination and the laying on of hands was led by Rose Becklin, associate executive minister. A song of dedication was sung by Susan Friedman, Rev. Ellison's sister. Bringing greetings was our Region president, Kandice Bailey. A dinner in Rev. Ellison's honor was held in the fellowship hall.

Entries such as these are often kept in bound record books. Keep in mind that these are not official minutes but are, nevertheless, documentary evidence that illustrate church life.

In the event that these entries are computer generated, print them on good quality paper. If possible, use acid-free paper, complemented by acid-free folders and storage boxes for all historical documents.

Preserving Historical Documents

Too often, old pictures are tossed into boxes void of identifying labels, or old minutes are stacked on a shelf in a closet. Just as common are previous clerks' records filed carefully away at home or passed on to a family member who no longer lives in the area. These are precarious positions for such valuable materials.

If this is the case in your church, advocate for permanent housing of your records and historical materials. Your records and those of your predecessors should be stored in a safe place. Provide security against fire, theft, water, insects, vermin, dust, and extreme changes in temperature and humidity. A fire-proof file cabinet provides minimal safety. A safe or vault is preferred. Or consider depositing the church records in a local archival facility. For more complete guidance on proper procedures for historians to follow, contact your denominational or local historical society.

Chapter 4

The Clerk as Correspondent

The clerk handles official correspondence on behalf of the church body: for example, letters requesting transfer of membership, notices of election and appointment, and letters of thanks, congratulations, sympathy, or invitation as instructed by the church body. If a church is large enough, an office secretary is employed to handle the pastor's correspondence and other routine matters in the life of the church.

Letters of Transfer

Whenever members want to join the church by transferring their membership from other churches, or when members leave the church and join others by letter, the clerk writes the letters. For the specific content of these letters, look at the materials you received from your predecessor or use the following samples.

If you use a computer, enter the text of the basic form letters into your word processing program. Give the letter a file name and save it for future access. With each letter you write, you will only need to make date, name, address, and pronoun changes. These letters should be written on church letterhead stationery. Keep a copy for your records. If you use the computer, print out a hard copy and place it in your record book.

Sample Letter Requesting Transfer of Membership *from* Another Church

Date

Inside Address

Dear Friends:

We are pleased that (name) has expressed his/her desire to join (name of your church). We look forward to welcoming him/her into our church family. We would appreciate receiving your letter of transfer.

May God continue to bless your ministry in (town).

Sincerely,

(your name), Clerk

Sample Letter Responding to a Request for Transfer of Membership *to* Another Church

Date

Inside Address

Dear Friends:

Thank you for your letter indicating (name)'s desire to join your church. We are pleased that he/she has found another church home. Upon your receipt of this letter, his/her membership is transferred.

May God continue to bless your ministry in (town).

Sincerely,

(your name), Clerk

Sample Letter Requested by an Individual Transferring Membership to Another Church

Date

Inside Address

Dear Friends:

(name), a member of (name of your church), has expressed his/her desire to unite with your church family. Within a reasonable amount of time following your receipt of this letter, our records will indicate this transfer of membership.

May God continue to bless your ministry in (town).

Sincerely,

(your name), Clerk

Notices of Election and Appointment

After an election, it may be the task of the clerk to notify officers of their election. (In some organizational structures, this becomes a closure activity performed by the nominating committee. Check with the moderator or pastor to see what is done in your church.) After business sessions where appointments have been made, it is the task of the clerk to notify the appointees and to outline the task to which they were appointed.

Of course, this should be done promptly. Keep a copy for your records.

Letters of Thanks, Congratulations, Sympathy, or Invitation

From time to time you will be directed to express thanks, congratulations, or sympathy, or to offer an invitation to sister churches on behalf of your church family. Follow standard rules of etiquette to write these letters. As you write, keep in mind that you are the church family's letter writer.

Chapter 5

The Clerk as Publicist

Publicity takes many forms. In general, publicity is the process of transforming information into public knowledge. It may involve giving legal notice of the upcoming business session. A simple announcement to that effect as required by the constitution and posted on the bulletin board will accomplish the task.

Publicity may involve print media: a press release to the local newspaper or a news article for the Region's publication. In these instances, you are calling attention to an event, promoting your church, or inviting press coverage. The challenge is to be effective. Here are a few helpful tips to help you do a good job:

- Include the five "Ws" and the "H" in a news story: who? what? where? when? why? how?

If you can, cover all six in the first paragraph. However, clarity is the test. Don't force all six into the opening paragraph if doing so results in clutter—too many words and long, complex sentences. Imagine your news story as an inverted pyramid with the essential facts at the top and the less important details at the bottom.

- Check everything for accuracy, then check it again! Pay particular attention to names, addresses, dates, titles, and basic facts. If you are using a word-processing program, use the spell-check feature, but recognize that it will not point out words that are spelled correctly but used incorrectly. In addition, ask someone to proofread what you write.
- Feature people. People like to read about people—themselves and others. Mention names whenever you can.
- Use 8½-by-11-inch sheets of white paper. Double space your copy, using only one side of each piece of paper.
- Identify yourself as the contact person for the news story. Include your address and telephone number.

Conclusion

Many workplaces employ the word "clerk" in their job titles. There are clerks of court, supermarket clerks, hotel clerks, county clerks—and the list goes on. Like many of the clerks in these varied workplaces, Don, a church clerk, describes his job as "an awesome responsibility."

He's right; it is! Take it seriously, all the while keeping your eyes open for the serendipities along the way.

Now that you've read this book, take some time to become comfortable in the role of church clerk before you pass judgment on the work assigned to you. Ask questions, consult with other leaders in your church, and examine the ways previous church clerks completed their tasks. Then it will be time to get some hands-on experience.

If you are fitted for the job, you will find enjoyment and a sense of purpose in your new role. There will be some unexpected pleasures, too. Keep track of the insights you gain. When your term ends, pass those insights on to your successor as well as the records that have been entrusted to you.

The work of the clerk *is* an awesome responsibility. Do it well; others are depending on you.

Related Resources

The "Work of . . ." Series
from Judson Press

The Church Business Meeting, R. Dale Merrill. A concise, readable guide to conducting business meetings.

The Church Newsletter Handbook, Clayton A. Lord Jr. A how-to guide for pastors, church secretaries, and active laypersons who want to create or improve their church publications.

Church Officers at Work, Revised Edition, Glenn H. Asquith. Suggestions for Baptist lay people who have been appointed to or seek responsibility in the service of the church.

Work of the Church: Getting the Job Done in Boards and Committees, David R. Sawyer. Creative techniques for "directed servanthood" that move congregations from faith to positive action. Includes help for placing people in appropriate positions, setting committee goals, adapting leadership styles, building the official board into a cohesive team, improving communications, efficient allocation of the pastor's time, and more.

The Work of the Church Treasurer, Revised Edition, Thomas E. McLeod. A complete, simplified accounting manual with each procedure fully illustrated for the new church treasurer or financial secretary. Especially helpful for the small church.

The Work of the Church Trustee, Orlando L. Tibbetts. This comprehensive guide covers every facet of responsibility.

The Work of the Deacon and Deaconess, Harold Nichols. An experienced deacon addresses those who aspire to this responsible calling.

Work of the Pastoral Relations Committee, Emmett V. Johnson. A guide to show how churches can bridge the communications gap between pastor and congregation.

The Work of the Sunday School Superintendent, Idris W. Jones, revised by Ruth L. Spencer. A helpful guide for the Sunday church school superintendent, outlining his or her responsibility as both a spiritual leader and a Christian educator.

The Work of the Usher, Alvin D. Johnson. A complete guide to ushering. Suitable for individual or study group.

The Work of the Worship Committee, Linda Bonn. For churches that want to be more thoughtful about the way they worship.

The Work of the Pastor, Victor D. Lehman. Provides basic information on the job description of the pastor.

The Small Church in Action Series
from Judson Press

Activating Leadership in the Small Church, Steve Burt. Explores the unique interaction between pastor and congregation in the small, close-knit church. Especially helpful are twelve guidelines for assessing small church ministry, mission, and programming.

Christian Education in the Small Church, Donald L. Griggs and Judy McKay Walther. Field-tested plans for achieving quality Christian education with limited resources include new ideas for tailoring programs to community needs, designing a curriculum, selecting resources, building relationships between education and worship, equipping leaders, and much more.

Developing Your Small Church's Potential, Carl
S. Dudley and Douglas Alan Walrath. Dynamic
possibilities for churches struggling to survive de-
spite dwindling memberships and population
changes. New ideas for making positive use of
community transition, absorbing newcomers into
the church family, reshaping the church's image,
resolving cultural conflict, and developing programs to reflect community needs.

*Making It Work: Effective Administration in the
Small Church*, Douglas Alan Walrath. Challenges
the assumption that administration in small
churches is either unnecessary or impossible.
Readers will learn how their ministry of administration can lead to an effective and efficient organization while being faithful to the nature and
mission of the small church. Also included is an
appendix containing a guide for using computers
in the small church.

*Money, Motivation, and Mission in the Small
Church*, Anthony Pappas. An on-the-job under-
standing of the small church culture, what motivates
members, and fund-raising ideas. This practical
guide shows pastors and lay leaders how to de-
velop big-impact mission projects with limited resources, provide pastors with fair compensation,

tap new sources of funds for building maintenance, plan realistic budgets, and much more. Includes a questionnaire to help pastors evaluate the "small-ness" of their churches.

For additional information, please contact Judson Press Customer Services, 1-800-458-3766.

Additional Church Record Resources from Judson Press

Church Roll and Record Book

This expanded version features space to record alphabetically the names of members and includes an additional 160 pages for minutes. There is ample space to record alphabetically names of church officials, auxiliary presidents, church affiliations, weddings, baby dedications, funerals, and annual summaries of membership. #55-0272

Record Cards

Application for Church Membership: A complete record card for new church members or those transferring from another church. Includes believer's pledge and the four requirements of vital church membership. #55-0030

Decision Card: Statement for new members to sign showing whether the person is joining by baptism, letter, or Christian experience. #55-0023

Certificate of Church Membership: Extends the hand of Christian fellowship to new members. Includes relevant scripture selections. #53-0011—KJV, #53-0012—NRSV

Wallet-sized Recognition Cards: An appealing way to recognize new members. Tastefully designed wallet/pocketbook cards give members a sense of belonging and pride in their identity with the ministry of their church. #55-0032

Letter of Transfer

Pack includes letters of transfer and notification to advise the original church that the member has been received into the new fellowship. Space is provided for a personal message about the member to help the receiving church guide the new member in finding a place in the ministry of the church. #53-0013

Items may be ordered by calling toll-free: 1-800-458-3766.